THE SPIRITUAL NOMAD CALENDAR

THE SPIRITUAL NOMAD CALENDAR

An Introduction to Lifting the Veil for Soul Empowerment and Soul Connect

Theresa Savanah Dion

Copyright ©2023 Theresa Savanah Dion

All rights reserved. No part of this publication may be reproduced, stored in a retrieval system, or transmitted in any form or by any means-electronic, mechanical, photocopying, and recording or otherwise—without the prior written permission of the author.

To perform any of the above is an infringement of copyright law.

For further details about services offered, to book a speaking engagement or to request permission to use any parts of this publication for commercial use outside of brief quotation, email your request to:

uprooted@coachingsurmesure.com

www.coachingsurmesure.com

Cataloguing in Publication (CIP) for this publication is on file at Library and Archives Canada.

Author photo by: Carlos, Art of Headshots, Vancouver Studio, British Columbia, Canada

Cover Design by: Iqra Jamil

ISBN: (eBook/.epub) 978-1-7752167-3-5

ISBN: (eBook/Kindle) 978-1-7752167-5-9

ISBN: (soft cover) 978-1-7752167-4-2

Table of Contents

Acknowledgement 1

Introduction 2

How To Use Spiritual Nomad Calendar 5

Disclaimer 7

Sunday Day One 8

Monday Day Two 10

Tuesday Day Three 12

Wednesday Day Four 13

Thursday Day Five 15

Friday Day Six 17

Saturday Day Seven 19

Sunday Day Eight 21

Monday Day Nine 24

Tuesday Day Ten 27

Wednesday Day Eleven 29

Thursday Day Twelve 31

Friday Day Thirteen 33

Saturday Day Fourteen 36

Sunday Day Fifteen 38

Monday Day Sixteen...40
Tuesday Day Seventeen...42
Wednesday Day Eighteen..46
Thursday Day Nineteen...48
Friday Day Twenty..53
Saturday Day Twenty-One......................................57
Sunday Day Twenty-Two...61
Monday Day Twenty-Three.....................................67
Tuesday Day Twenty-Four......................................70
Wednesday Day Twenty-Five..................................74
Thursday Day Twenty-Six.......................................78
Friday Day Twenty-Seven.......................................82
Saturday Day Twenty-Eight....................................84
Sunday Day Twenty-Nine..87
Monday Day Thirty...91
Bonus Section..94

ACKNOWLEDGEMENTS

I would not have been able to complete this work without the support and encouragement of my dear soul friends Gael White, Carol Beaudet and Henrique. Thank you for your continual encouragement and patience. It means more to me than you will ever know.

Thank you, Gael, for taking the time to revise, proofread and provide me with suggestions during the editing process.

I also want to thank my children, Liliane, and Scott, for bringing up aspects of myself that are hidden deep within my soul and would not otherwise be brought to my consciousness to be healed and reconciled with, should it not be for their only presence in my life. You are my breath of life.

I dedicate this work to all the beautiful souls who seek to unite with their spiritual nomad essence and be soul empowered.

Introduction

Hello and Welcome beautiful soul. I am so glad you have chosen to explore the essence of your spiritual nomad qualities within yourself.

During the 30 days period, we will focus on different aspects of our life and align more with the spiritual nomad within we all have. It is here we're following our heart to know where our soul begins.

First let me introduce myself, my name is Theresa Savanah D. I am an author, spiritual coach, a spiritual nomad at heart and passionate about ancient civilizations, particularly the Neolithic era.

Other passions that merged gradually over the course of my life are astrology, ancient philosophies and healing techniques. (Did you know that ancient civilizations used the stars to monitor the healing process of someone, or that Vedic astrology is still used today in India for the understanding of compatibility in marriages?).

However, the anchor of my spiritual growth has been my dreams and the symbology and metaphor they contain. I still recall dreams from the time I was a little girl and have received teachings over the course of my life on the meaning of their metaphors and symbology, along with wisdom from the Divine Source and my guides. The spiritual nomad essence and its qualities came to me in my dreams over the course of a transitional time of my life. The teachings I received were to support me during that transformational experience and now I am grateful to share it in this work with you.

In addition I have learned different languages, some of them basic, to help during transitions I went through over the course of my life. This I called uprooting and shared more in my first book titled - <u>Uprooted 8 Ways to Reinvent</u> <u>Yourself and Reignite your Passion for Life</u>. I've lived in different Canadian provinces, in Europe for 7 years and travelled extensively in Europe and some parts of Latin America.

But my fundamental passion and soul Divine life mission is helping you to ignite within your spiritual nomad essence as we lift the veil for soul empowerment and soul connect.

My hope is that as you explore and discover the unique essence of your spiritual nomad you will find blessings and gratitude as you uncover some aspects of yourself. All this while moving forward with self-exploration and adventure that lies within your spiritual heart – your soul.

The Spiritual Nomad… Where exploration of self and adventure unite…

How to use the Spiritual Nomad Calendar

Here you will find a layout over the span of 30 days, containing sections to explore different aspects of your life along with suggestions to integrate and align with your soul, your spiritual heart, (the seat of the soul.)

I suggest you take a moment during your day where you can spend about 30 minutes for self-exploration. There are no rules to follow, just your spiritual heart and its guidance, keeping in mind that the seeds you plant will grow because of consistency and commitment to yourself.

Why 30 days and not 15 or more? Because research has shown that whenever we begin something, may it be an exercise program, a habit of some kind it usually takes about 21 days for it to integrate and become a routine.

Each exercise will focus on a day of the week and I suggest that if you miss a day, simply change the day so you keep with continuity. For example, you miss a Tuesday and resume on a Wednesday, then make the Wednesday a Tuesday and so on.

You will also notice that each day is numbered so you can easily keep track.

What do I mean by spiritual heart? Where the soul lives, where the fire of life we all have within resides. Where intuition whispers its wisdom.

Wherever you are on your spiritual journey, by letting the essence of your spiritual nomad within guide you, aspects of the strength it carries will be unveiled and if you allow its qualities to guide you, transformation will take place.

You can find more details of my work and who I am on my website www.coachingsurmesure.com

Blessing and Gratitude from my soul to yours.

May the spiritual nomad exploration begin.

Disclaimer

The purpose of the Spiritual Nomad Calendar is about self-exploration and is not intended to provide any form of therapy. We all have free will in making choices and decisions about our life, the approaches and suggestions provided in the calendar are to assist on your spiritual journey.

The author is not liable for any misinterpretation, decisions or actions taken or resulting from the suggestions and exercises included in the calendar.

The results and transformations that are possible reside in you. It will depend on your personal commitment to your journey.

Sunday - Day One

The calendar begins on a Sunday because intuitively, it is a day that we have been let's say, programmed on a collective level to rest.

Today the focus is where you are on your journey. It is important to take a hindsight look periodically at what actions we habitually take and choices we make that lead us to where we are in the present. In other words where are you at now, in all aspects of your life, may it be personal relationships (including the one who have with yourself), work related, financial, and social.

In the space below, take the time to self-reflect on these areas of life and where your spiritual journey is at. Everything that takes place in our life reflects not only the choices we make but also what takes place at a soul level. The soul is the compass that guides our path, so in the end, when we do our work, the soul completes its journey in the intended Divine mission and purpose it was given. There is a fundamental reason why you are here at the present time and the reason is solely for the soul's evolution.

Describe for yourself what areas of your life you are thriving and where you are not by asking yourself:

-What are some choices I have made that brought me where I currently am?

-What are the results and what would I do differently now that I see in hindsight and why?

There is no need to dwell long on this Day One, keep in mind that when it comes to your spiritual journey everything has a purpose. This should not take more than 15/20 minutes. Just be honest with yourself, it is your process and no one else's. Use the blank space below to write or use a journal of some kind for the duration of the calendar. Research has shown that whenever we learn something, writing it down helps us to integrate what we are in the process of learning.

I will see you on Day Two – Monday.

Monday - Day Two

Today's focus is self-care. In the busy and distractive-filled world we live in it is easy to forget about ourselves, forget about our essence. Our ego or monkey mind often wants to keep control and throw us off our spiritual path. It is clever in making us believe at least trying to, that it knows best in this world to have and have not.

One of the essences of the spiritual nomad is to be able to differentiate when it is coming from the ego and when to use self-care no matter what is taking place. Like engaging with the dance of life, while being aware of its distractions and setbacks and moving forward with equilibrium without losing sense of self. In other words, going through the experiences that life puts on our path while remaining conscious of all choices we are required to make.

Is it coming from my ego or my spiritual heart-my soul, wanting me to move in that direction?

In the space below, describe for yourself what you perceive the soul and the ego to be. We all have a definition.

-Describe one or more situations where you know you followed one over the other? Do you tend to follow mostly your ego or your soul?

-How did you feel? Were you able to know the difference or did you make a habitual choice based on another similar situation?

Take the time you need. It is not a contest nor a race.

I will see you on the Third Day - Tuesday

Tuesday – Day Three

Today's theme is about equilibrium, inner equilibrium. We all have what I call an inner compass that helps us to stay on the path. The compass is felt and experienced via our intuition, and it is where the innate wisdom of our soul communicates to us. The soul has a blueprint that it needs to follow given by the Divine Creator, which builds on the foundational purpose of why we are here at this time. This purpose is often clouded because of what some of our beliefs are and the societal expectations that are put upon us.

It is of value to us that we connect with this soul driven purpose, this Divine given mission that has been engraved in our spiritual heart, in our soul.

Take a few minutes to ask yourself the following questions:

-What is my true soul purpose? Why am I here?

Name it in one word. (As an example, for me it is to individuate - to break free from the collective.)

-Have I ever known what it is? Or have I just gone in whatever direction seemed to be the right one?

- Do I normally ask my intuition for guidance? Or do I just have an immediate reaction?

I will see you on the Fourth Day – Wednesday

Wednesday – Day Four

Today we focus on forgiveness. It is easy to believe that we are capable of forgiving something that took place in our life or even to say we have forgiven someone else. However there is often a misunderstanding of what actual forgiveness means. True forgiveness means that by doing so I allow myself to not give my power away to something or someone and thereby allows me to feel more at peace. Another layer of energy behind the power of forgiveness is that it allows me to break the chains that may bind me.

The most challenging thing we are called to do at times in our life is to self-forgive also in return. The spiritual nomad has an innate sense that the power of co creation resides within one and for the soul teaching to come forth one must also self-forgive. Easier said than done I totally get that.

As an introduction to what forgiveness means for you, ask yourself the following questions:

-What is my definition of forgiveness?

-Can I say I have done so throughout my life? How did it feel? Do I tend to keep grudges or hold on to anger, or do I experience peace and acceptance of being a co-creator of the situation?

-Describe a time where you used forgiveness and have forgiven yourself in the process? What was the outcome? How did you feel afterwards?

I will see you on the Fifth Day – Thursday

Thursday – Day Five

Today's theme is about comfort zone and its limitations versus growth. We all have a place where we find comfort. It is often sought in the way we live, our relationships, and what we are familiar with. It is a form of security and with time often will bring the energy of stagnation and growth, spiritually speaking.

We gravitate often to our comfort zone because without being conscious, our ego likes to remain in control and that is a perfect way for it to do so. For the spiritual nomad essence, being outside of familiarity and comfort is an ordinary part of life. Even if at times the need to gravitate toward it is manifested and even so it is not limited to how and when. The spiritual nomad essence knows intuitively that the soul is always in evolution which requires being out of one's comfort zone.

Ask yourself these questions to help determine how often you have or find yourself outside of your comfort zone:

-Which situation or experience can I say I was propelled outside of my comfort zone? What was the reason? Was I able to find comfort outside of my comfort zone?

-On a scale of 1 to 10 (1 -none, 5- sometimes, 10 – being a regular way of life) have I been truly outside of my comfort zone?

-What propelled me there? At a soul level there is never a coincidence.

I will see you on the Sixth Day – Friday

Friday – Day Six

Today is about creativity. The basis of creativity and being creative is where we can manifest something. We are constantly creating in our actions, in our thoughts, with our emotions. These are components of ourselves, and we rely often on our five faculties to guide us. We like or dislike something which nourishes and makes us feel a certain way.

The essence of the spiritual nomad knows that the words, the thoughts, and actions all contribute to shaping the impact and the result of the creative energy we put forth, consequently contributing to the collective consciousness as well as the individual one. It starts with the self always. The words, the thoughts, and actions we carry will impact either in a desired or not so desired way.

The spiritual nomad is conscious of creative energy and being self-aware is not something that one will abstain from. The spiritual nomad knows intuitively of the impact it will have.

To understand more about where you are at when it comes to the creative process ask yourself:

-How am I aware of my thoughts, my actions, my words, and the impact they have in my life and how it makes me feel? Describe one or two situations that highlight your awareness.

-Do I self-correct when I realize the energetic impact they may have?

I will see you on the Seventh Day – Saturday

Saturday – Day Seven

Today's theme is about who you are. That's right. Our soul is here for its evolution, we take on a role and a personality to support us in experiencing our spiritual journey, so the soul can have the experience through us. Each day we present ourselves with an identity of what makes us who we are, or at least think who we are. We are a person of course but the question is, how do we present this personality. We look in the mirror and see someone, yet we are more than that.

On a spiritual level, we are a soul created by the Divine Creator who came here to fulfill some kind of purpose that has been preassigned. We live this purpose in our beliefs, our philosophy of life, in the choices we make in our daily lives via the spiritual nomad qualities we have if we give it permission to.

The qualities we all have are what make us. They are the glue that keeps us together, where the light of the Divine shines and from there we can share that light to this beautiful world we live in.

As an introduction to whom you truly are, write down how you view yourself. Keep it positive, speak from your light that is beaming from your

beautiful soul, your spiritual heart. Give space for your intuition to guide you through it.

-Who are you? What are your qualities? What are your strengths and weaknesses?

-When you see yourself in the mirror, how do you perceive and think of yourself?

-Are there thoughts that come up? Be still and listen as the answers are within.

I will see you on the Eight Day – Sunday

Sunday – Day Eight

Today's theme is to go a little deeper into the very first day of a week ago, Sunday Day One.

The reason for this is for you to unleash and connect more at a soul level where you are at and where the qualities of your spiritual nomad essence are fundamentally. Go back to what you have written about the areas of your life and what lead you there. Take a moment to revisit that day.

There is no right or wrong when we focus on life being a spiritual experience.

Pick an area of your life where you felt accomplished or currently feel so.

Maybe it relates to finances, work, relationships. This is the positive aspect of your hindsight.

Now write down every aspect of the area of life where you feel you are living your full potential, where you feel emancipated by asking yourself these questions:

-What quality in myself have I unveiled in this area of my life that makes me feel I am living to my full potential. One word only.

-Did I choose courage? Trust? What was it?

The importance of identifying the quality you used magnifies the vibration of that word and the connection with your spiritual heart.

Whenever we feel we are living our full potential in an area of our life, we were guided to draw from within a quality of our spiritual nomad essence. Our soul thrives when we are living to our full potential.

An example for me, one area when my soul thrives is when I go and explore different places in this beautiful world. Another one is when I write. A quality I draw forth is trust, trust in myself and in my soul.

Then see if you can come up with 2 other areas of your life and do the same exercise.

Now choose an area where you feel more change needs to take place, where you are not living to your full potential.

-Is it more self-care? Perhaps more loyalty to your soul? How do you perceive yourself in general? Do you feel like you deserve it? What is it?

-Again with one word put a quality that speaks to your spiritual heart, allow your soul via your intuition to tell you. What quality is needed in cocreating that change so it can support in transforming that area of your life.

An example for myself I must keep working on is self-forgiveness.

The qualities you identified now can become an invocation for you. Make a commitment to yourself that whenever your journey brings you to a similar situation or choice, these qualities you have can help in strengthening your alignment with your soul and be soul empowered. I will see you on the Ninth Day – Monday

Monday – Day Nine

A good part of this week we will look at some qualities we all have which may be buried or fully alive within our spiritual nomad essence and today is an introspective look at courage.

Courage comes when we are aware of a fear that binds us from doing something but we do it anyways. It is a quality we all have if we allow it to guide us. It empowers our connection with our soul. When we use the quality of courage to propel us we experience soul empowerment as we need courage to assist us in some kind of transition for a transformation to take place.

It is not unusual to bury the quality of courage because we know we will be propelled outside of our comfort zone. I'm sure you have heard or may even said '' I wish I had the courage to do that"

Courage can be needed in different areas of our life, whenever a transformation of some kind is needed for the soul's evolution. Throughout my life I have been told I don't know how many times that I am someone that has courage. At times I have not felt I did but when I reflect on some phases of my life when I was totally outside of my comfort zone I can see I needed to have courage in order to move forward.

Courage acts like a compass within coming from the soul's guidance, our spiritual heart.

When we decide to be courageous, it's like creating a domino effect within our energy field and it becomes easier to accept when the need to be outside of our comfort zone comes up, thereby becoming more empowered at a soul level. Being outside of our familiarity of life is not easy as we lose the sense of remaining in control. Courage is a quality available within each of us if we allow ourselves to be soul empowered.

Take time today to explore different aspects of courage and its impact it has, or had, in your life by asking these questions:

-When was a time where I needed to be courageous to move forward with something? Which area of my life have I needed to be action oriented?

-What does courage really mean to me?

-What was the outcome?

-How often have I used this quality when I found myself outside of my comfort zone?

-Do I more often choose not to be courageous?

-On a scale of 1 to 10 (1-never, 5-sometimes, 10-always) how often do I allow myself to be courageous when the need is felt?

I will see you on the Tenth Day – Tuesday

Tuesday – Day Ten

Today we look at what the quality of trust really means for us. Trusting can have a double edge energy behind it. Let me explain what I mean by that. We are often conditioned to give our trust away to something or someone else outside of ourselves and in return we get some kind of let's say, benefit. By that I mean that when we don't follow our intuition, it is easy to give our power away to a particular thing or someone without even questioning it within ourselves first. We all do it or have done so throughout our life.

However, trusting in oneself is a different thing and for that we need to have full awareness of the benefit of its quality. Lacking trust in life and oneself is not unusual because again, when in trust, we know at some level that the need to let go of control will be required.

When we are in trust however, we merge with life's synchronicity and our soul's evolution. Things flow and the sense of being alone subsides. <u>In my book, Uprooted – 8 Ways to Reinvent Yourself and Reignite Your Passion for Life</u>, I go into more details of how the quality of trust at a soul level came forth as

I was getting ready to travel to Greece to research ancient civilizations.

The spiritual nomad essence necessitates to be trusting as one's inner boundaries are constantly challenged when it comes to being soul empowered. In a way trust and courage are tied together as we first need to have courage and trust in return when a transformation is about to take place.

To explore this quality within ask yourself these questions:

-Am I someone that normally trusts myself first and checks with my inner wisdom beforehand, my soul, my intuition?

-When was a time in my life that I truly trusted myself? What was the outcome? What propelled me to be aligned with the quality of trust?

I will see you on the Eleventh Day – Wednesday

Wednesday – Day Eleven

Today's exploration is about self-responsibility. In other words, accountability in being a cocreator of one's life. This is somewhat tied to the second day where we explored self-care.

For the spiritual nomad within taking responsibility for one's life is something that comes with its lessons, trials, and tribulations. It is not always easy to say the least as the societal conditioning allows us often to give our power away. However self-responsibility entails that the spiritual nomad not only follows the soul's guidance via intuition but also takes ownership of the energetic self that comes with it.

The essence of the spiritual nomad knows that the actions, the words, the thoughts and what is felt on the inside will reflect directly and indirectly in the physical reality we live in. We have the power of cocreating. Self-reflection and questioning work together simultaneously and the exploration of how being energetically responsible will have a ripple effect not only on the individual consciousness but also on the collective.

Each day we are called to take part in the world we live in but how we contribute to it is where this quality can support us in creating from our spiritual heart.

To explore this quality, ask yourself these questions:

-What is my definition of taking self-responsibility and how does it reflect into my daily life?

-Do I allow my thoughts to run freely? Do I go into reaction instead of action when something takes place?

-What about my emotionality? Do I tend to allow my e-motions to dictate?

-How can I unleash the power of cocreating and of self-responsibility as I follow my soul's blueprint as Divinely intended?

I will see you on the Twelfth Day – Thursday

Thursday – Day Twelve

Today's introspective look is about freedom. Freedom like success has a unique definition for each one of us. We seek freedom financially, in our choices, our life, with our relationships, and so forth. However in the context of the spiritual nomad essence freedom goes much deeper than this. Freedom acts like a liberator of our whole energetic being that comes and lives in what we perceive as reality as well as within our energetic field like our thoughts, choices, actions.

The meaning of freedom also varies for each one of us hence the uniqueness of its quality.

Freedom to the spiritual nomad is about feeling a higher sense of purpose and integrating it while honoring the soul's evolution and its Divine blueprint.

It is in a way related to the fourth and fifth day about forgiveness and comfort zone where self-liberation of the chains within that binds us are removed. It is where we feel soul empowerment.

We all need to know we are free, which is a God given right, and the soul seeks experiences to have its own evolution. The essence of the spiritual nomad knows that everything begins with self, the awareness of what limits and restricts one to move forward (one's inner barriers) so one can experience what freedom truly means within.

Letting our thoughts run wild, our emotions to dictate our reactions are also what can cause our inner barriers to limit the uniqueness of what true freedom means for each one of us.

Freedom, a word that has different meanings for each one of us but for the spiritual nomad essence it relates to breaking the inner barriers that limit us from following our spiritual heart- our soul.

To explore what freedom means to you ask yourself these questions:

-What is my definition of freedom? What do I perceive or believe freedom to be?

-Do I idolize something outside of myself and let it define what freedom is?

-Which area/s of my life can I say I am free? (There is always one.) When something no longer serves me, do I feel soul empowered to change it and make a choice or action to cocreate the change? Do I mostly follow my intuition in that process, or do I move in reaction just because?

I will see you on the Thirteenth Day – Friday

Friday – Day Thirteen

Today we look at loyalty, a soul-searching approach of what it means to be loyal to oneself which will create a ripple effect in one's life.

The question is whom I have loyalty towards. The essence of the spiritual nomad thrives in being loyal to one's spiritual heart, to one's soul.

In our daily life, we tend to be loyal to something or someone. We can be loyal towards the people we work for or with. In our personal relationships we are loyal to our beliefs and perceptions until we choose otherwise simply because we are convinced they are true.

But here the introspective look is about oneself and what it means to be loyal, to follow one's spiritual heart, one's soul.

The spiritual nomad essence intuitively follows the signs that life puts on the path, aligns with its message, and goes inward for intuitive clarity to assist in making a change of some sort that will contribute to the soul's evolution.

The signs can come in a myriad of ways such as the sentence of a book, the message of someone, the sudden presence of a pet, an occurring of some sort, a feeling.

The spiritual nomad knows that there are no coincidences, that whatever takes place is for the soul's evolution, that it is part of its Divine blueprint.

Loyalty to the soul is like seeking to understand by intuitive reflection.

It's about being loyal to the Divine mission given to the soul. We all have one. We have heart desires and mind desires, loyalty in this case resides in the choice made to follow the heart first over the other.

In other words, to think with the heart instead of the head.

Explore this quality aspect within yourself with the following questions:

-How do I define being loyal when it comes to my spiritual nomad essence? Do I or have I followed more my heart over the course of my life or more my ego's short term so-called desires? What is the difference for me and how do I know?

-Do I see or feel myself separate from the occurring/s in my life? Do I believe in coincidences? Or do I follow the signs given in life's synchronicity?

-Describe a situation where you did not believe in coincidence and were following the signs that life put on your path?

-Do you seek to intuitively understand something first?

I will see you on the Fourteenth Day – Saturday

Saturday – Day Fourteen

Today's exploration is about vision quest. A vision quest is often seen and done within certain North American Native tribes and normally last four days and four nights. I would also add that some of the ancient civilizations had their own form of vision quest that carried on for generations, where the initiate was left with one's vulnerability to explore the inner world that resides within. It can also be done as a rite of passage of some kind during the initiate's life span.

(The Spartan civilization, for example, had initiation rituals for the boys around the age of 7 to eventually become warriors).

For the spiritual nomad, time spent alone and being with oneself can also be described as a vision quest because of the recurring need to detach and turn inward as he knows that the compass resides within. In other words knowing when to turn to the quietness within, disconnect from distractions that keep the mental active and sensing when one's energetic field is saturated is a building foundation of connecting with one's soul.

Sitting in quietness and turning everything off to BE with oneself can be challenging when we begin to explore our inner world and connect with our soul, however it becomes easier as we follow our spiritual heart.

It feels like a wave coming from intuitive guidance, like a deeply ingrained need that surfaces, when the necessity to connect with one's vulnerability becomes a priority.

There is a difference between being by yourself and BEING WITH YOURSELF

Explore this aspect of yourself by asking these questions:

-How often do I sit in quietness and BE? Am I easily distracted by my thoughts? Can I be impartial and simply let them be? Are they simply passing by because they are just thoughts or, do I easily give in by responding to them?

-Do I like BEING with myself without any form of distractions? Can I turn everything off and just BE?

-How comfortable am I with myself? In my vulnerability? Describe a time when you felt vulnerable. What took place and how did that make you feel?

I will see you on the Fifteenth Day – Sunday

Sunday – Day Fifteen

First congratulate yourself, give yourself a big bear hug as we are now halfway to the end of our time together. I'm sure by now you are aware of the different qualities that your spiritual nomad essence carries within and how the transformation of integrating them has begun on some level.

So, *Bravo* for the commitment towards yourself.

Around the twentieth day we will move into a more sensible approach so we can focus on integrating deeper with our soul, our spiritual heart.

But for today let us look at humbleness. Humbleness stems when we allow ourselves to be vulnerable. The essence of the spiritual nomad knows intuitively that when we tap into this quality, life flows easily and we feel more serene. We are more serene because we easily embrace aspects of ourselves instead of trying to suppress them. We live in humbleness when it comes to understanding that our soul has a Divine mission to follow and through humbleness comes authenticity. Authenticity of who we truly are at a soul level and this reflects in our immediate reality. (It's like stepping beside ourselves as we let go of our ego trying to keep control.)

Humbleness permeates all aspects of our life as our spiritual heart shines its light. We find as a result more fluidity in our life, things happen, synchronicity takes place, and our gratitude grows because we are fully aware of the power that results from being humble.

Life leaves us with a WOW feeling.

To explore this quality, ask yourself these questions:

-Do I allow humbleness to permeate my life? How comfortable am I in my vulnerability in general?

-How easy is it for me to let go of control?

I will see you on the Sixteen Day – Monday

Monday – Day Sixteen

Today we look at the quality and the art of letting go. Letting go of what no longer serves us, letting go of something that took place. In other words, letting go of something that hinders us to move forward. Remember the quality of forgiveness earlier? When we can let go it is because energetically we are more at ease to forgive and to self-forgive. They have a, let's say, energetic inter dependance relationship.

Since the spiritual nomad essence is humble towards what is needed at a soul level for its evolution then the need to let go comes at a point of not being a choice but a necessity for the soul's evolution.

The essence of the spiritual nomad intuitively knows that the ego likes to remain in control and one of the ways is its inability to let it go easily. This is especially so if it means the ego has to become humbler for the soul. One of the ways to identify if letting go takes place in our life is to notice if our mind no longer gravitates to that occurrence, that situation it was grasping onto, that our thoughts towards that very same occurrence no longer dominates. It can surface at times but we are no longer influenced by it. We no longer give our power to it.

The need of letting go relates and influences most aspects of our life including work, financial, relationships, material objects, furry friends, and most importantly our comfort zone.

To explore your ability of letting go ask yourself these questions:

-Can I easily let go of something or someone in my life or do I tend to hang on?

-Is there something that I still allow my mental and my ego to influence me by hanging on to it?

-Do I attach myself easily to how things are supposed to be or can I move forward even if it is challenging to do so?

-Is there something in my life I need to let go of? Name it and ask your intuitive wisdom how you can do so, what is needed from you? Is it a material aspect of your life? A toxic relationship?

The need to change something with work? What is it?

I will see you on the Seventeenth Day – Tuesday

Tuesday – Day Seventeen

Before we begin today, I'd like to remind you that nothing in the approach of the calendar is about going out of our way to push energetically for something to happen. The essence of the spiritual nomad knows that when we open ourselves to this inner connection, we all have we naturally unite with life's synchronicity.

It is about learning to connect more with the qualities of the spiritual nomad self, to trust and follow our spiritual heart and our soul that speaks to us via our intuition. The calendar is a work of many years of not only self-exploration but also guided via intuitive wisdom. As I shared earlier, dreams have been my spiritual anchor and the sharing in the calendar stems from years of not only personal experiences to allow this spiritual nomad essence within to emerge but also comes from my own trials and tribulations of aligning with those teaching over the course of many years. We can all allow guidance from our spiritual nomad essence to come forth, some qualities and approaches may differ for each one of us as our individual journey differs. We may find that some qualities are already active within while some may need to be refined. Our soul's blueprint is unique yet these qualities are ingrained within each of us allowing guidance from our spiritual nomad essence.

Today's exploration is about the art of detachment. Being detached from the should and must can be a challenge however is needed especially when it comes to following our spiritual heart and the blueprint of our soul.

Detachment can be easily misunderstood by most of us making this quality a lifelong experience not only because of the misunderstanding we may have but mostly due to the expectations that are put upon us especially at a societal level in how things are supposed to be.

Detachment is also tied with many of the previous qualities explored in the calendar. For example, if we are to detach we need to practice letting go, to find inner equilibrium, to practice self-care, to merge with creativity, to go inward with a vision quest… You get the idea.

Detachment of how things are supposed to be can leave us perplexed because it often requires us to be outside of our comfort zone in whatever area of our life is needed.

Detachment also brings on the ability of differentiate what is needed when it comes to the e-motional (energy in motion) stagnation of a particular aspect of our life as some qualities are unveiled to better unite with our spiritual nomad essence.

For example, I often had to detach from my comfort zone and the predictability of life and allow my spiritual nomad to thrive and explore. In other words I need to be somewhere physically so I can have the full experience of what is needed at a soul level in order to integrate for my evolution. Not everyone is like this and I'm not saying it must be this way. This is part of my uniqueness.

However, our spiritual nomad essence is intuitively aware that detachment from how it is supposed to be is part of the process when we are moving towards soul empowerment. In whatever aspect of our life, it may be required we can do this more easily when we allow ourselves to be receptive.

And the beautiful part is that it often comes when we are compelled to, when we allow inner guidance from our spiritual nomad essence.

When life throws a curve ball, we are often called to detach from how something or someone is supposed to be. Detachment also can entail an emotion, a belief that has made us feel or see it should be a certain way.

To explore this quality within, ask yourself these questions:

-Do I most often prefer my life to be a certain way, or I am often compelled to make a change of some sort where detachment is needed?

-Do I tend to intuitively know when I must detach from something or someone that is creating toxicity in my life, may it be a relationship, a financial situation or perhaps work that no longer helps me evolve?

-Do I often feel stuck in life? Do I have the sense that something is weighing me down?

-What does detachment or being detached mean to me? What is it that I feel the need to detach from? Describe it.

I will see you on the Eighteenth Day – Wednesday

Wednesday – Day Eighteen

Today is dedicated to taking a retrospective look at what has been done until now. We are moving into a more everyday approach to help us integrate deeper the essence of our spiritual nomad by revisiting some of the answers to the questions we have covered so far. Perhaps you have some of them that you need to dive into more or go over some of the days for a clearer understanding. So go ahead, make notes, refine, rewrite, choose again.

We will use the qualities we covered in the calendar towards integrating with our spiritual nomad essence to better assist us with gradually feeling more serene and subsequently have more fluidity in our lives.

As you re-read and revisit these last 17 days, make a note of what you want to change or enhance in your life. Is it financial, relationships- including with yourself, a personal project, work related?

See if you can pick 3 main areas of your life where you need to make a change or enhance. Write down 3 to 5 qualities (that we covered in the calendar) which you feel are needed to support you moving forward. From now until the end of the calendar we will work towards sustaining the shift and integration of the spiritual nomad qualities you have chosen for yourself.

Allow your intuitive wisdom to guide you. This is not a mental exercise but a soul aligned exercise, a spiritual heart exercise.

I will see you on the Nineteenth day – Thursday

Thursday – Day Nineteen

To move into a more practical way of integrating the essence of the spiritual nomad thus allowing our soul to guide us, we first need to believe we can create a change in our life. It is all about believing. In order to change something, we first need to believe it is possible. One of the ways to assist us is to change the perception we have towards that very same thing.

Let me explain what is meant by this. When we are called to make some kind of change, we not only need to detach from the perception we so dearly hang on to, but we also need to shift our belief that anything is possible. Miracles happen daily and it is possible to shift our perception for the change to take place. It all begins with deciding to do the action.

When we act we are giving permission to ourselves that we not only believe it is possible but also that by doing so, the essence of our spiritual nomad intuitively knows that the perception will shift simultaneously. Because we are more dependent on our five faculties, we need to see something to believe and it can only happen with taking action to create that shift.

Let's take a common area of life. Finance. Money like any other aspect of our life is an energy that needs to be circulated however the choices we make with how we use that energy are where some of the qualities can help us.

When it comes to money we all have given our power away at one time or another in exchange for some kind of benefit, for example a compulsive purchase. We may also perceive ourselves not worthy of having it, believe there is not enough to go around or that having money is bad.

Yet at the same time we can choose to live beyond our means, to spend it before we earn it or we hold the perception that because all is fine today we will be fine tomorrow.

In addition, the energetic stagnation that often comes with our finances is fear and the need to keep control. Controlling the what if that comes with short and long term.

We worry about not having enough, worry about losing our comfort zone, worry about how we will be able to enjoy life. The belief of lacking and not having enough becomes the driving force. It is like a paradox. At times we perceive we will be okay no matter what, other times we fear not having enough that we are not worth having it. The other side of the spectrum is we have been blessed with having plenty so we don't need to worry.

Money is used as an example but as you can see, other aspects of our life also relate to a perception we hold towards making a change. It can relate to a fear of not having someone in our life if leaving a toxic relationship. A work situation can drain our energy as we keep giving our power away because we believe we will not find something better. The perception and belief we hold towards something creates a direct impact on our quality of life.

The good news is that when we shift our belief and in doing so are influencing our perception about something, we feel compelled to decide and take action to create the change needed by allowing some qualities of our spiritual nomad essence to surface and being committed towards oneself.

For example, we need courage to commit to making that conscious choice, we need loyalty in our commitment to make that change and we may need to do a vision quest to allow guidance from our spiritual heart to take place. We need self-care and self-forgiveness for past choices we may have made or detachment of how things are supposed to be.

If we have convinced ourselves that our perception and belief are true, then making a change may feel like going against the tide when it is the opposite. Some questions to explore for intuitive clarity if doing a vision quest are… Is this my truth? Is this what I truly believe in? Is it truly how I perceive it to be?

Take a moment to choose an area of your life you wrote down on day 18 and one or more of the qualities you have chosen for yourself.

Then to support yourself in doing the action and to experience more serenity and fluidity in that area of your life, work with the following:

-What is the belief/s or perception I carry about _____ (fill in the blank with the area of your life). Is it missing my sense of comfort zone? Is it the lack of? What is it? Identify it.

-What do I need to change my belief? In my perception?

-What action do I need to take, what is the commitment needed to allow my spiritual nomad essence to support me?

- Am I willing to be open to the quality needed? What is my perception and belief about following my spiritual heart, my soul?

-How willing am I to shift my perception about that very same thing?

I will see you on the Twentieth day – Friday

Friday – Day Twenty

Today we look at the importance of defining needs and wants. For the sake of congruency and since the energy of money is a foundation of our life, I will keep using it as an example however, don't hesitate to apply today to other areas you have chosen for yourself.

For the spiritual nomad essence needs are very different than wants especially when it comes to the soul's evolution, our Divine mission, and the reason why we are incarnated at this time.

Needs are something that build on the soul's evolution and since the soul requires certain pre-determined experiences to continue its evolution, it will have these experiences via the essence of our spiritual nomad.

At a soul level wants can be more of a deterrent from the needs because when they come from the lower self the ego, wants we believe we have can take us away from the true requirements of the soul's needs. In other words it's about being able to discern the difference between these two by allowing our spiritual nomad' s qualities to guide us. Let's explore this further.

The needs and wants normally work together. To keep it simple however, by allowing the essence of our spiritual nomad to bring us intuitive clarity thereby to align with the soul's needs, we simultaneously tap into some of the qualities we covered.

For example, to help distinguish the purpose behind the need of wanting and having we gain clarification by doing a vision quest for us to become more aligned with the synchronicity of life by trusting. This results in moving forward with letting go and allowing the spiritual nomad's guidance so we align with our soul and become soul empowered.

The reason why I use money as an example is that we are often in the want energy which may not necessarily be what the soul needs for its evolution. It is not unusual for us to be in our ego and push the energy for something to happen and live for example beyond our means such as compulsive buying. The ego likes to play monkey mind instead of believing that in due time it will take place if it is in alignment with the soul's needs, the spiritual heart.

What is required of us is to be in action (based on the needs rather than be in reaction because of the wants) and believe because our perception of time often brings a delay when it comes to the Universe in what is meant to be. Think about this for a moment. Do you always get what you want? Common response is no, but we do get what we need. All in due time.

The essence of the spiritual nomad distinguishes intuitively the difference between these two and will put forth the want however, with the detachment of when and how, by allowing the soul to bring it forth, if it is what it needs.

(It's easy for us to believe that because we don't get what we want right now that it will not be, but the idea is to shift our perception and believe that even our wants will happen in Divine timing and does not require us to push the energy.)

We are influenced by the collective of how things are supposed to be and learning to know the difference between these two helps the spiritual nomad essence to guide us. The soul becomes more empowered by connecting with what it needs, thus feeling more aligned in the choices we make.

As a result, we can experience more fluidity in our life and feel more serenity within when we are in alignment with the soul's needs.

To understand more the difference when it comes to the needs versus wants of being soul empowered, ask yourself these questions:

-Do I often react when I see something, or do I make a mental note of it and explore within if it is what my soul needs?

-Do I know the difference between what my needs and wants are?

-When was I able to follow more what I needed, instead of being tempted by? Describe a time when you were able to do so?

-Do I feel a sense of being not worthy when I don't get what I want? How do I feel when that happens?

-When I make a choice, do I go within and ask for intuitive clarification from my spiritual nomad's essence? Or do I just move into reaction?

I will see you on the Twenty-first Day – Saturday

Saturday – Day Twenty-One

Today we look at making choices. Conscious choosing that is. Up until now, we have seen different qualities and have begun to see how we can use these aspects of our spiritual nomad essence to merge and align with our soul, to be more soul empowered.

For today and because making choices encompass all aspects of our life, it will be feasible to the ones you have chosen, may it be relationship- including the one with yourself, work, social, food, financial, even being out of your comfort zone, because making choices is required in all areas of our life.

We are faced daily to make choices, at times out of reaction (our wants) other times because we feel within it is a necessity (our needs) thereby feeling compelled to. The beauty is that we have the power to make choices that serves not only the collective, but our individual process and we have the power to make a different choice.

Ironically, we at times are often unhappy with the choices we make, with how things unfolded and yet at the same time, we feel disempowered in making a different choice because we have no idea how or where to begin. The good news is that nothing is written in stone. There is always a choice such as not choosing is a choice, or choosing something to do when we feel the need to say no but we do it anyway. This is also an indication that we can choose differently by following our intuition and saying no.

Because all choices we make create an energetic ripple effect in our life, it is good practice to align with some qualities so we experience more serenity within and feel the power behind the choices that life presents us with.

For example, we often need to work with forgiveness for past choices we may have made, we require self-care and be loyal to the choice we now decide to make to create a change for the better, and we require creativity to make the change.

In a nutshell all choices entail some kind of action. The decision of not making a choice remains an action. We decide to act on not making a choice, just like we make a choice to change something that no longer serves us. When we are called to make a choice, it brings with it a change of some sort. However, because of our tendency to have expectations or being ambiguous of the choice we must make, it can be much easier to not make a choice, hence not taking action to create the change.

In addition, because making a choice can bring uncertainty resulting in us having to decide to remain in our zone of comfort. It can create a sense of stagnation in our life, as if something is pushing us to remain in our comfort zone.

When we choose to allow things to remain as is because of a fear, conscious or unconscious, we may very well have the experience that things don't go as smooth as they could. This may lead to the sensation that something within is nagging us to make a choice for the energy of stagnation to be released, at the very least lessened.

For example, we choose to remain in a work situation that no longer fulfills us because of the financial situation we may have created with previous choices we made. We need to make a choice daily of what we are going to eat, with whom we are going to mingle with. Yet, some choices that often come last are commitments with us in making conscious choices and aligning with our soul, using the spiritual nomad's qualities to help us with intuitive clarity.

We forget that we have the power to choose and when we choose consciously it is because we can more easily differentiate between what is needed at a soul level versus what is desired, as these will equally create a consequence, a ripple effect in our energetic field which leads to manifesting what we perhaps are not wanting to create instead of what is needed.

Just like the saying that says… ''choose wisely''.

To further assist and help with where you are at and to better consciously choose, ask yourself these questions:

-Which aspect of my life do I tend to delay making a choice and I know something must change? - Is it with my finance? Social life? Self-care? What is it? Identify it.

-Do I tend to hang on to a relationship of any kind that I know drains my energy?

- What is it that I fear the most when it comes to making choices? Is it losing my comfort zone? Is it change? Identify it.

-What do I need to be able to make more conscious choice/s? What is the quality I need to draw from my spiritual nomad essence? Name it.

I will see you on the Twenty-second Day – Sunday

Sunday – Day Twenty-Two

Today we look at how everything is an extension of our energetic field. The choices we make, the perceptions we hold, the beliefs that allow or stop us from moving forward. So essentially, it's all about energy because as we have seen, the way we think, the words we speak, the actions we make, e-motions we have, all create a ripple effect and move from energy to manifesting in our life, collectively and individually and can contribute to remain in our mental sphere instead of moving towards our soul.

We often hear that we are spiritual beings having a physical experience, so, if that is the case, then we need to be fully conscious of every energetic resonance taking place within. In other words, being responsible for what we put out to the world we live in.

Everything that surrounds us, our material belongings, our friends, the work we choose to do, act like a mirror in our life and we often see ourselves separate from them. Yet they are like a guiding post.

For example, let's take our vehicle. We have an e-motional attachment to it whether we are conscious of it or not. It takes us from point A to B, we use it for work purposes consequently bringing income to our life. We use it to get away on vacation, road trips, and so forth.

The place we live in is also a reflection as it echoes the comfort we like to go to, brings pleasure in our life, we decorate it to be visually pleasing, we organize it to be practical. The point I am making here is that everything we have in our life is an energetic extension of ourselves, may it be our food preference, social, relationships, etc.

The spiritual nomad essence energetically discerns that everything is an extension of oneself and therefore it is easier to attract what is based on the needs rather than the wants by connecting with the soul. It puts forth what it would like, uses detachment from the how and when for the soul to manifest it in one's life. Let me give you an example.

I was without a car for two to three years after I returned from living in Europe as I lived in the city and used my bicycle and public transport to get around. That is what was needed at the time because I was still in a transition and intuitively knew that where I was, it was temporary, so to keep things simple it was the best choice life presented me with. I could have bought a car and ignored my intuition, however due to the circumstances I was not going to follow my ego's wants and push the energy. Instead, I did a vision quest and connected with the qualities I needed like courage, loyalty, and trust to support me in the transition I was in.

Sometime later, I moved and at that point, my spiritual nomad essence knew the need to manifest a car was coming up. I could energetically feel it. Consciously I put out what my preference (want) was about the type of vehicle I wanted to attract and I used the quality of letting go because I knew that coming from the spiritual nomad essence, I was in alignment with my soul and all was going to be perfect as it always is.

A few months later, the perfect car showed up. A neighbor was selling his wife's Toyota which was good with fuel consumption, low mileage, well taken care of and within the price range I had put forth in my preference. What I did not realize is that a few months later, I needed to have the car to take the road across Canada. The trip took me six days to get to my destination with no issues whatsoever. Because this trip was part of my soul's blueprint, that this road trip was needed before I consciously did, the manifestation of the perfect, safe car came with ease. All in life's synchronicity.

Making this move was part of my soul's evolution, so it had to take place.

My soul path is drawn out like that, not everyone is, and I am not sharing this to make a point that it is supposed to be this way. Yours is unique to you. However, whatever is happening in our life, it is an extension of our spiritual nomad essence and being conscious of the responsibility we hold is how we can manifest and align with life's synchronicity and be soul empowered while being in our spiritual heart.

Our mind often tries to make us believe we must have it now, but as mentioned earlier, it can lead to be in reaction instead of blending with life's synchronicity to bring the right moment to move into action.

The energetic extension applies to all aspects of our life and if we connect with the qualities of our spiritual nomad essence while being fully conscious, we connect with life's synchronicity. It is not about pushing the energy but doing what is needed at a soul level. In the example I shared, the car was needed for me to take the road trip as part of the soul's path.

That is where the difference lays. Everything is an energetic extension of ourselves. A desire or want (reaction) may not necessarily be what the soul needs in that phase of our life or in that moment in time.

When it is part of the soul's Divine purpose it will be manifested when we are ready to welcome it, because we are conscious of the energetic extension our spiritual nomad essence has with it.

To better clarify and understand what is needed for you when it comes to the presence of energy in

your life, ask yourself these questions:

-Can I say that I am aware of my own energy? Can I feel the energy I give out in my thoughts, actions, words, and the choices I make?

-How conscious am I really? On a scale of 1 to 10 (1 -never, 5- sometimes, and 10- always) where do I rate myself in being aware of my energetic extension?

-Do I see myself separate from my surroundings and my material objects? Have I ever seen my car, my house, the clothes I wear as an energetic extension of myself? Or is it just another thing?

-How aware am I of the relationship/s I have in my life? Do I tune in to my spiritual nomad essence and ask what is needed or do I just think I can have it now?

-Did I have or currently have recurring issues when it comes to my vehicle, my house, my work? And if so, what do I need to do about it? Name it.

I will see you on the Twenty-third Day – Monday

Monday – Day Twenty-Three

Today we look at intention, the basis for all creation. The beauty of intention is that when we are conscious, we can feel its power. Let's explore this further.

We hear I would even say that we tend to create clarity when it comes to our intention. By that I mean, we'll clarify something we said or done like ''it was not my intention to hurt your feelings'' or ''it would never be my intention to'', or ''I intent to make that move I have been delaying making''… you get the idea.

From a philosophical perspective, it's as if our intention reflects the consciousness that drives our actions, our thoughts, our words, even the way we may feel. What if intention was like consciousness in action at that moment? Good question to ponder for sure.

We also carry an intention when we need to create something, like a project, find work, establish better relationships, when we want to change something by creating a shift, we need to have intention to be able to move forward. For our creative energy to guide us.

Intention is also an embodiment of several qualities of the spiritual nomad essence. For example, we need to believe we can, we need to allow creativity to flow through just like we need self-responsibility in putting out the intent because like anything else, it creates an energetic ripple in our life. We require loyalty and humbleness when clarification is required.

As you can see, having intention envelops being conscious in our actions, with our words, and our thoughts because of the domino effect it creates, individually and collectively.

Ironically it is also a deeply ingrained aspect of ourselves, like a veil of awareness that is buried deep within each of us. When we choose to be fully conscious, we come from this inner wisdom we all have rooted in intention, our power of creativity. At the same time, we may not have clarity in our intention when sending out mixed messages in our energetic field that may lead to confusion, lack of determination and so forth. We all had this experience.

Whenever the spiritual nomad feels a sense of confusion within, a vision quest may be the route to go to bring clarification, by consciously asking questions like why, when, how, as the spiritual nomad essence connects with the spiritual heart, the soul for guidance.

The essence of the spiritual nomad also knows that when living in the spiritual heart, the soul's Divine mission will be filled with intentions in creating experiences just as it is Divinely intended. (Reread this last phrase and feel the power behind the words.)

To better elucidate how you naturally connect with your intentional creativity within ask yourself these questions:

-When I feel a choice is about to take place in my life, do I connect with the essence of my spiritual nomad essence for intuitive clarity, or do I just make the choice without connecting?

-Do I experience confusion and lack of clarity upon making a change of some sort? If so, what led me there? Did I ask for clarification with how, why?

Write down some qualities you know you connect with intuitively when it comes to intention. Define these qualities in what they mean for you and identify how they have supported you when it comes to intentional creativity? Make a commitment with yourself to connect within first before passing into action.

I will see you on the Twenty-fourth Day – Tuesday

Tuesday – Day Twenty-Four

The power of being in the present moment is the theme for today. But before we proceed, take a moment to reflect on how you are feeling since you began to connect and explore the spiritual nomad essence in you. Is there a shift within, an awareness of what needs to be refined or awaken more in you? The spiritual nomad is about inner awakening to connect with your soul by using the wisdom and the qualities that lays in its essence.

This is not a linear exploration of yourself. The themes of the calendar are a result of many years of not only following the qualities and the essence of my spiritual nomad with the self-exploration it brings, but particularly in the teachings received in my dreams. As this work is shared with you, I am too, in a way, self-exploring further by doing the exercises and I am grateful to do this journey with you.

We are now in the last week of the calendar and don't forget to give yourself a bear hug for coming this far.

Today's theme is about exploring the power of being in the present moment and its importance. We are continually influenced by thinking about the future while at times the future is blended with something that took place in the past. We all have that experience. We plan, we project something from the past or into the future, we at times are unsure about the future so we prefer to remain in the past with certain beliefs, certain ways of life as we allow ourselves to be influenced by the collective and our own ought to. I get it.

In a way it is all about what may or may not take place, how history may repeat itself (unless we have learned its life lesson). It's like a melting pot that resides in our mind without discerning which concoction it may result in, except for the spice of familiarity in it.

Being in the present moment does not mean to not desire a better future for ourselves or to explore the inner growth that took place. It means that to be in the present moment we allow ourselves to be in a place of serenity within. Some ancient philosophies, like Hinduism, say that when we organize our mind, when we put all these compartments of our thoughts, e-motions, words into an aligned state, when we learn to not interact and allow a thought to flow in and out without giving it attention, when we give ourselves permission to do this with everything that takes place within, we can experience more serenity within and in our surroundings.

In other words, it reflects outward.

Being present in the moment, working towards inner serenity takes loyalty to do something that will assist us in refining being present, like sitting in meditation or prayer, for example, or taking a walk alone and leaving our phones behind. Being in the present moment is to take deep breath as we let go when we feel pulled inside to interact with our monkey mind, our thoughts, our e-motions. Being present in the moment is when we allow a vision quest to guide us, in finding this inner center we all have, it is when we find inner equilibrium.

Ancient teachings all seem to return to the same point. When we focus on being in the present moment, our mind is organized and it creates a ripple effect where only the now becomes real, what I call soul empowerment, because we can see clearly what we need to do, to choose, to move towards.

It is moving beyond the mental sphere and move instead into what is also called the Void… It is about lifting the veil of the monkey mind and open the door to being soul empowered.

To better define how being in the present moment is for you, ask yourself these questions:

-Do I normally allow my mind to wonder in any direction? Can I say spending time with myself in quietness, without distractions, is something I do regularly? Or do I allow my mind to sway me in whatever direction?

-What is it that stops me from being alone, without distraction? Do I find it challenging to do it? Do I thrive on being mentally active?

-What quality/ies do I need to bring forth from my spiritual nomad essence to help me find more serenity?

- What action/s do I need to commit to so I can be more in the present moment?

I will see you on the Twenty-fifth Day – Wednesday

Wednesday – Day Twenty-Five

Today we look at reorganizing our life from within and turning our weaknesses into strength.

Up to now, we have covered different aspects that are part of the spiritual nomad essence. We all have them, some of them buried, some are very much alive. We use them at different times throughout our life depending on where we are at and what is taking place. When we commit ourselves to follow our spiritual heart, our soul, we gradually move closer to our Divine mission, the reason why we are here, intended by the Creator, God.

How do we do that, organize our life from within you may be wondering. Each time we turn inward for guidance, it becomes easier to decipher what is taking place. Then we need to sort out the needs from the wants to better connect with our intuition, our spiritual heart. Like sitting in quietness to leave the distraction of the five senses and allow our breath to take us deeper into ourselves, helps us reorganize within, because the breath is our life force. It is the first inhale we take at birth and the last exhale when we transition. Deep breathing and connecting within is the basis to be able to sense what is taking place so we can move to the next level within.

Think about this for a moment, how often do you stop and take deep breaths? For me when I feel a stress come up, taking a deep breath calms my solar plexus which is a point of reactivity for me. And from there, I can connect more with what is taking place. Is it a fear of some kind, is it my mind playing tricks on me? Am I too much in the future of what may happen? (All these amongst others inner disturbances contribute to being disorganized within because our mind likes to play monkey tricks on us.) Then it becomes a ripple effect within, my mental slows down, and my solar plexus stops reacting.

For you it can be different when you sense that a reaction from within is taking place. It can be to stop and be still for a moment and you become aware of what is taking place. Or it can be that doing something like being in nature, looking at a plant, talk to your furry friend, will help to move you forward in awareness.

So, how do we turn a weakness into a strength? First step is awareness of the why we identify it as a weakness. To someone else it can be viewed as a strength but when the need to reorganize ourselves from within arises, we can easily view it as a weakness. We all have done it. Hence comes the importance of asking ourselves what is needed. Let me explain.

The qualities of the spiritual nomad essence we have seen are to each one of us, a strength, or a weakness, at some point in our life. It either needs refining or it is a quality we often use, that we rely on to propel us forward.

To better assist with what is required to reorganize your life from within dive into these aspects of your life and define what quality you use the most and the one/s that need refining. Don't hesitate to review exercises up to now, if need be, especially what we covered on days number 5, 8, 11, 13, 20, and 21.

-Financial: what do I need to do when it comes to my financial sphere of life? What are my strengths (identify 2 qualities minimum) and how are they helping me move forward?

What are my weaknesses (identity 2 qualities minimum) and ask your intuition what is needed to turn them into strength. What is needed for them to be refined?

-Do the same for the sphere of your life that relates to work, social, relationships – including self-care.

-What are you committing to, to reorganize your life from within with what you identified as strength and weaknesses? Do you need to take a deep breath? Cuddle with a fury pet? Go in nature? What is it you need when it comes to reorganizing your life from within?

I will see you on the Twenty-six day – Thursday

Thursday – Day Twenty-Six

What a journey this exploration of our spiritual nomad essence has been. Hopefully you have written down the exercises in a journal of some kind, reviewing them or perhaps a need of redoing the calendar at some point can be very much part of the continual journey when connecting deeper with our spiritual nomad qualities, moving us towards soul empowerment. Life is a journey not a destination. However, when we are loyal to our soul's evolution, we can feel more serenity within as we move forward in our life's magnificent journey.

We constantly change in our awareness, thereby influencing our evolution as we integrate the spiritual nomad's essence within.

Today's introspective look is understanding the importance of unifying the neutrality of the Divine. What do I mean by that? To simplify it, there is no division, only perception.

The whole purpose of the calendar is to break the chains that bind us, to bring more awareness with whom we are and our unique life path, our soul's Divine mission and to, last but not least, use a practical approach in understanding who we are and how our words, thoughts, actions, beliefs, perceptions can contribute to being disorganized within when we allow ourselves to follow our mind, our ego, in lieu of committing to follow our spiritual heart, our soul.

It is also to be aware that pushing something that is not readily meant to be will often deter us from being in the present moment, that it will impede our ability to decipher the difference of the soul's needs versus the ego's wants whenever a choice is required nor to allow detachment to take place from our perception of what we believe something to be.

In other words, we need to think more with our spiritual heart instead of our head.

Have you ever conceived the idea that when we choose to be aware of what we perceive a situation to be is part of the perception we hold towards that very same thing? That by choosing to shift into a more neutral way, in other words of not letting specifically what I perceive something, a situation, even a person to be, it is easier to move into what is called a Divine neutrality, thereby bringing compassion to the perception of what we see or believe.

Imagine it like putting the car in neutral gear, I can still hear the motor, car is ready to move forward until I decide to remove it from neutral. Divine neutrality is to abstain from judging what we perceive something to be. Divine neutrality helps us to shift our perception and belief from judgment and move towards allowing it to be, to let go and let God.

Divine neutrality helps us remain in the present moment, to not be a savior or try to convince others otherwise, to not push our perception and judgment. Divine neutrality is something that we are all capable of moving towards, and we can do that as we work towards soul empowerment, as we follow our spiritual heart, our soul, because the soul is whole and within the Divine consciousness...

To better assist with what Divine neutrality is and how it applies in your life, asks yourself these questions:

-Can I say that I am often judging something I perceive or believe to be? What is my initial reaction? Do I tend to be closed minded instead of open minded?

-What is my initial reaction when someone comes to me and shares something that is taking place in their life? Do I move into savior mode?

-What does being a savior really mean to me?

-What comes up for me, internally when I see something taking place, do I go right away into judgment? Do I react by not believing it or knowing better?

-What action or thought can I choose to help me move towards Divine neutrality? Create a word or invocation when you feel pulled into judgment that deters you from being in the present moment like…

I choose to _____
(fill in the blank with a thought or a mantra) whenever I perceive or judge someone or something.

(An example can be, I choose to not judge and remain in the present moment) or can be something like (I choose to not be the savior and allow this person to have the experience) … you get the idea.

I will see you on the Twenty-seventh Day – Friday

Friday – Day Twenty-Seven

As we come towards the end of the thirty-day calendar, changes within have already been taking place, as minute as they can be, simply because you have committed yourself this far to connect deeper with your spiritual nomad qualities.

Today we are going to review so tomorrow we can write a letter to ourselves, connecting with our spiritual nomad essence. This helps to put together how far we have gone, our awareness of what we need to refine and what our strengths are.

Writing a letter to our spiritual nomad helps us to integrate more its qualities as we move towards being soul empowered.

Before we can do that, I invite you to re-read and define which area of your life you feel the need to integrate more as by now you have become more aware of yourself.

Which area of your life do you need to commit when it comes to following your spiritual heart, your soul.

Is it financially, socially, work related, self-care, be more in the present moment, move towards Divine neutrality, shift your thoughts, learn to let go, to detach? Is it with making conscious choices? To practice forgiveness and self-forgiveness?

Allow your spiritual nomad essence to guide you. Take your time. You may need to take a bit longer while you define the sphere/s of your life. You may want to take a walk-in nature to help you with clarity, to meditate, to use bullet points in your writing. Whatever you need to bring clarity.

So go ahead, allow creativity to guide you.

I will see you on the Twenty-eight day – Saturday

Saturday – Day Twenty-Eight

Today is the day we write a letter to our spiritual nomad essence. Keep in mind that there is no right or wrong as all is experience, it is your life, and a beautiful one that is. All that has or is taking place is a gift to move you closer to your Divine mission, your soul's purpose.

When we give ourselves permission to integrate the qualities of our spiritual nomad essence, to allow our inner compass of the soul to guide us, life becomes simpler. We gradually are able to remain in the present moment, to see clearly the choices we are to make, to detach from the should and wants of the mind and allow ourselves to be guided from our spiritual heart, our soul.

The ups and downs, the experiences we all have don't necessarily go away but it is our ability to deal with them that changes. Instead of being swayed by the e-motionality that life may bring, we are able to return to that place within where we find ourselves connected with the essence of our spiritual nomad. From here we are able to move forward with clarity and compassion of self and others.

The letter to your spiritual nomad is not written in stone. Because we are continually evolving in awareness, the letter can be written and rewritten as many times as you are feeling the need to do so. It's just like redoing the calendar or specific days may be needed. Simply trust whatever or whenever your intuition is guiding you to do, it is life's synchronicity speaking to you.

Hopefully sharing my letter to my spiritual nomad will help you get started…

A letter to my spiritual nomad essence

I know I have not always been following your guidance. I have at times allowed my mind to play tricks on me and have made choices that now with hindsight, I would have made different. I have occasionally kept as priority the belief of knowing better. I would say that my biggest weakness of your qualities is to allow my e-motionality to take over more often than necessary.

As you also know, because you are the foundation that brings me closer to my spiritual heart, my soul. I have dedicated my life to align these weaknesses within, to have trust in your guidance and use your qualities intuitively throughout my life.

In the last thirty days I have learned a lot more about myself and today as I write You This letter, I commit to be still and intuitively follow your guidance. I commit to be loyal to my soul's Divine mission and when I deter from it, that I allow my mind to try and convince me otherwise, I will take deep breaths, be still and intuitively listen first. Following your guidance and using these qualities within Will strengthen me on my life's journey. I will keep building up my courage and trust in myself and life. Each day as I wake up, I will set the intention to connect with the inner compass of my soul to guide me and allow synchronicity of life to take place allowing it to guide me throughout my day.

You are me, and following my spiritual heart, my soul, is the Divine reason I am here.

Sincerely, Me…

I will see you on the Twenty-Nine day – Sunday

Sunday – Day Twenty-Nine

How are you feeling?? What transformational process has taken place within? How do you feel?

Life is a journey and each day brings an opportunity to connect with our soul. All we are required to do is give ourselves permission to do so, it is about intention.

We talked about the power of words, thoughts, actions, beliefs. We covered qualities we all have within our spiritual nomad essence. We have self-explored where we are in our life, what needs to be more awakened, refined, blessed also. Because knowing where we are on our journey, our evolution, helps us strengthen the essence of our spiritual nomad.

Today is the day before the end of the calendar. Great work and wherever you are on your journey and exploration of yourself the past 30 days, it is all perfect as it is divinely meant to be.

It is not a race, when we learn to embrace each day as part of our experience, our world changes because we are changing ourselves inside first.

There is no quick fix or savior that will make everything go away. Life happens for a reason, it throws us curve balls, has ups and downs, makes us heal parts of ourselves.

It can be difficult to celebrate or embrace life when we find ourselves in turmoil. Believe me, I've had my share of challenges. From severe back issues as a teenager, left to myself from the age of 10, and the list goes on, having to learn how to be me has been quite the journey. What I came to realize is that even if I tried to be different, it did not work. I have never really fitted in the mold to begin with, and trying to go against that and be normal, whatever that means, is totally against who I truly am. At times I have tried to go against my spiritual nomad essence, especially when called to be out of my comfort zone, only to realize that it was easier to connect with the qualities I needed to support me in that transition.

I have been uprooted (talk about this more in my book, <u>Uprooted- 8 Ways to Reinvent Yourself and Reignite Your Passion for Life</u>) more than one can do in a lifetime.

But in the end it is all part of the experience of my soul, and by strengthening the qualities of my spiritual nomad's essence, somehow it all worked just beautifully. Life synchronicity becomes apparent and intuitive clarity comes naturally.

It is dedicated work, but the rewards are greater.

So, BRAVO to you for being here, BRAVO to your life's experiences for guiding you to be completing the calendar. It is your process, but you are not alone. We are all walking the path, the trajectory or destination differs but we are all here for a reason, there are no accidents nor coincidences.

Trying to be happy is like living under the veil of illusion. We all have been there; we are conditioned to do what makes us happy. What about thriving to BE in joy instead, which is a state of the soul. Joy brings contentment and when we have contentment, we are aligned with our Divine purpose. Happiness will take care of itself because it co-exists within when we are following our spiritual heart, our soul.

If we thrive to be happy and follow our mind's expectations and ego's wants and needs, it cannot last because we can never fully satisfy the ego. The ego wants more, the soul wants quality not quantity.

We all have done something or acquired something where we thought it would make us happy, only to find out some time down the road that we are needing something else. What we initially believed would make us happy is not satisfying us enough. Whether we seek it in our relationships, work or finances we are conditioned to believe we need to seek happiness in one sphere of life. But when we are aware and make conscious choices, we intuitively feel contentment and joy as it is the natural state of our soul.

We are humans and by shifting our perception and thriving to be aligned more with our soul brings synchronicity in our life as we are uplifted with joy.

I will see you on the Thirtieth day - Monday

Monday- Day Thirty

What if you were to imagine what it would look like if you took your life back. What would you be doing, where would you be going, expanding on?

The key to the last thirty days is to merge with our inner wisdom and think more with the heart instead of the head. By doing so we will not only take our life back but we will find more equilibrium within ourselves.

Imagine this for a moment. What does a step in your life's shoes look like? What is your heart deepest desire? Are you mostly living in an illusion or in reality? Do you normally wait for something to happen or for some kind of sign as you focus on the future or the past? Or do you follow through when you decide on something? Deciding and taking action are key, as you align with the qualities of your spiritual nomad essence.

What do I mean by living in an illusion? Are you waiting for this something or someone to tell you which decision or direction to take? Or do you use these innate qualities to guide you? Is it easy for you to follow your intuition? Or do you mostly live in the mental sphere, in your thoughts?

What about finding inner equilibrium, following your soul's compass?

How grounded are you in the present moment? What do you commit to when you sense that the past or future is trying to dominate? Make a commitment with yourself to embrace the present moment today. This is not about neglecting the possibility of what the future may bring or what has molded your life up to now. This is about committing to think with the heart instead of the head, to remain in the present moment and welcome the grace each day has to offer.

It is putting on the shoes that you walk each day in and tie up the shoelaces. It starts with the self always. When was the last time you could say you did what was best for you so in return you are better equipped to assist others? Being self- ish when we come from the heart is different than coming from the ego's perspective.

This life is about you in a compassionate way. It is about letting go of what no longer serves you and open the door to the possibilities that are put on your path. It is about acceptance of what is beyond your control and making conscious choices of what you have control over. It is about self-forgiveness and loyalty to your life path, to your essence.

This inner equilibrium we all have access to.

I give thanks for doing this journey we call life with you.

May your life be filled with more miracles and blessings.

With love…

BONUS SECTION

The essence of the spiritual nomad is all about freedom, the freedom to merge with the wisdom of the soul. To let go and embrace the newness of what life brings.

It is not always an easy process, especially when we are called to face the dark side of our soul, our shadow, but the rewards are greater if we allow our reflection in the mirror to transpire.

We live in a world where busyness often takes over, we have drifted away from who we are at a soul level and allowed our mind to take over. It is however, our responsibility to keep our intention where we want our attention to go.

You may have heard the saying ''energy flows where attention goes''. The question is, are you choosing to remain in charge of your energy? Because it's all about intention.

The intention of knowing ourselves at a soul level, to think with and follow our heart instead of our head.

Decide today, make a commitment with yourself to overcome the inner barriers that are holding you back in whatever you are seeking. You are a creative being, just as the Creator has intended you to be.

Since our words, thoughts and actions determine the road we choose to take, make a commitment with yourself to speak a different language in your daily life. Make it now. Because…

Decision and action bring manifestation.

The Spiritual Nomad… Where exploration of self and adventure unite as we follow our heart to know our soul.

From my soul to yours,

Gratitude Always.

www.ingramcontent.com/pod-product-compliance
Lightning Source LLC
Chambersburg PA
CBHW050916160426
43194CB00011B/2429